Frogs and Toads

Words by Dean Morris

Raintree Childrens Books
Milwaukee • Toronto • Melbourne • London

Library of Congress Number: 77-8116

4 5 6 7 8 9 0 81 80

Printed and bound in the United States of America.

Library of Congress Cataloging in Publication Data

Morris, Dean.
  Frogs and toads.

  (Read about)
  Includes index.
  SUMMARY: An introduction to the various frogs and
toads, their physical characteristics, and their
behavior.
  1. Frogs—Juvenile literature. 2. Toads—Juvenile
literature. [1. Frogs. 2. Toads] I. Title.
QL668.E2M67   597'.8   77-8116
ISBN 0-8393-0003-4 lib. bdg.

This book has been reviewed
for accuracy by

Dr. Max Allen Nickerson
Head, Vertebrate Division
Milwaukee Public Museum

Frogs and
Toads

Frogs and toads can
live on the land or in
the water. We call
this kind of animal an
amphibian.

Most frogs have smooth, slippery skin. Most of them live in wet places. The frog in this picture lives in a marsh.

frog

Most toads have rough, bumpy skin. The little lumps all over their skin are called "warts." Toads usually live in drier places than frogs.

natterjack toad

The toad in this picture does not jump like a frog. It may even walk on all four legs.

It digs a hole in the ground and stays there during the day. At night it comes out to look for food.

Frogs and toads eat small insects and worms. Many catch their food with their long, sticky tongues.

When a frog sees a moving fly, it shoots its tongue out. The insect sticks to the tongue. In a second, the frog swallows the fly.

Most frogs have many small teeth. Most toads have very few teeth.

long, sticky tongue

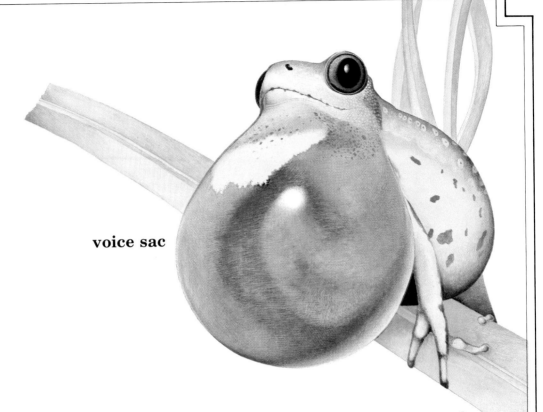

voice sac

In early spring you can hear frogs and
toads calling each other.

Most females' voices are not very loud.
Usually males make loud, low croaks. They
call without even opening their mouths.

Male frogs have voice sacs in their
throats. A voice sac is stretchy, like a
balloon made of skin. Some frogs have voice
sacs that swell up until they are almost as
big as the frog itself.

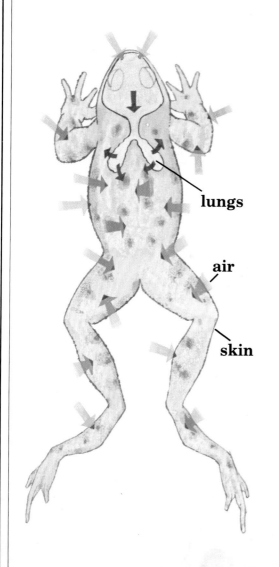

lungs

air

skin

Most grown amphibians have lungs for breathing, like people. They can also breathe through their skin. But the skin must be damp for the amphibian to breathe through it. An amphibian can die if its skin dries up.

As an amphibian grows, its old skin dies and splits. There is a new skin under it.

Most amphibians do not have strong teeth or claws to fight their enemies. But some have poison glands in their skin.

If an animal catches a toad in its mouth, poison flows out of the glands onto the toad's skin. The taste of the poison may cause the animal to drop the toad.

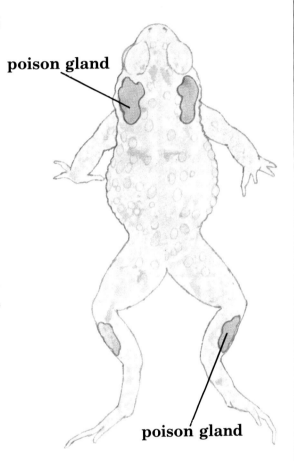

poison gland

poison gland

Some amphibians live in hot, dry places. This is a burrowing toad. It digs a hole in the earth or sand to keep its skin cool and damp. It usually comes out of its home only at night or after it rains.

If this toad does not feel safe, it may puff up its body like a balloon to scare off its enemies.

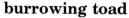

burrowing toad

Here are some "dangerous" amphibians.
The horned frog has sharp teeth.
The arrow-poison frog makes a very strong
poison. Indians of South America used to
put it on the tips of their arrows when they
hunted.

Dangerous animals often have brightly
colored skin. The color tells enemies
they had better not attack.

arrow-poison frog

horned frog

Cuban tree frog

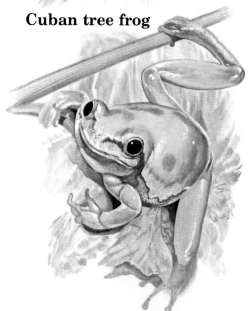

European tree frog

Some frogs live in trees. The long, padded "fingers" on their legs help them to climb.

The sound this Cuban tree frog makes is like snoring. The European tree frog is often kept as a pet. Its skin changes color. On sunny days it may be bright green. On cloudy days it often turns gray.

Most tree frogs are hard to see because their green skin is the same color as the leaves. Some tree frogs lay their eggs in trees.

The tree frog in this picture makes a nest of mud on the edge of a pond. A small pool of water fills the space in the middle. The nest helps keep fish from eating the frog's eggs.

Smith tree frog

Not all amphibians are frogs and toads. Newts are amphibians. One way newts are different from most frogs and toads is that they have tails.

This newt lives in ponds. It stays in the water most of the time.

This male newt has a frill on its back. This is called a crest.

female crested newt

The male newt grows this crest in the spring. The newt is a salamander.

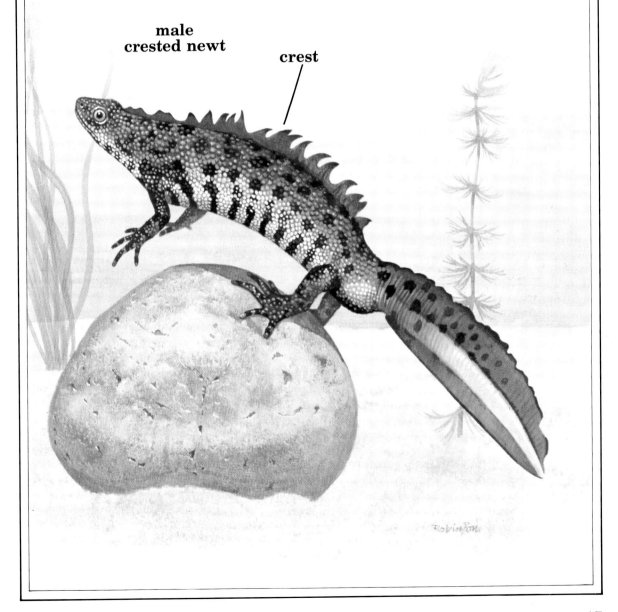

male crested newt

crest

Most salamanders are not newts.

Salamanders often have colorful markings on their skin.

This is a fire salamander. It lives in the woods. Sometimes it hides in logs or tree trunks.

Sometimes a person would put a log that had a salamander in it on a wood fire. The salamander would run out when the log started to burn.

People used to think that the animal had come from the fire. That is why it is called the fire salamander.

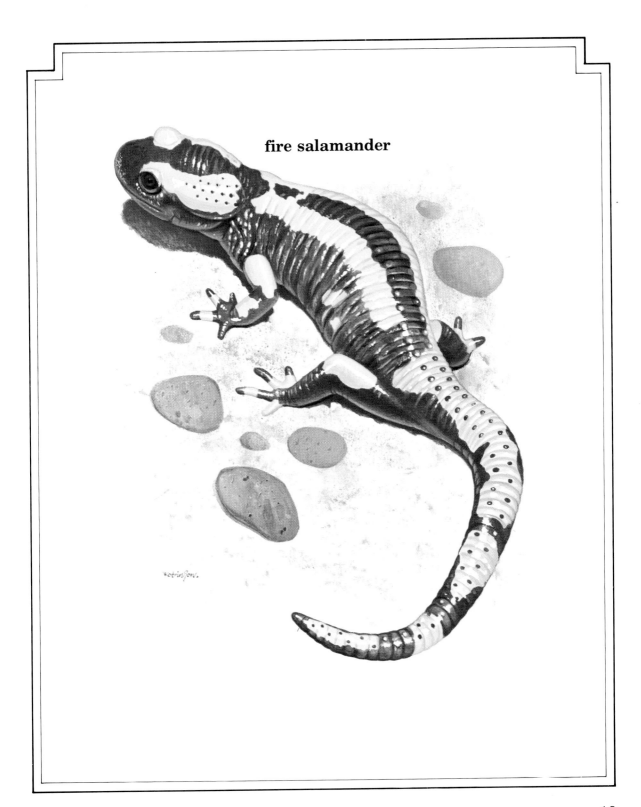

fire salamander

Most amphibians lay their eggs in the spring. Most of them lay their eggs in water.

The female frog lays lots of eggs. Each one has a ball of jelly around it. The eggs float in clumps on the water. The egg clumps are called spawn.

frog's spawn

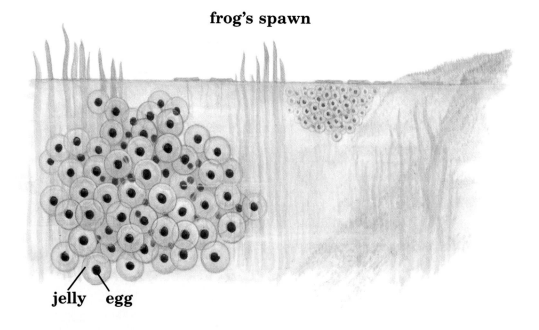

jelly egg

At first the eggs
have no eyes or mouths.
After a few days the
eggs turn into tadpoles.
They hang onto plants
with their suckers.

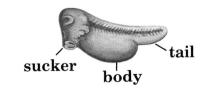

Soon gills grow on
the tadpole's head.
The tadpole breathes
through these gills
and its skin while new
gills grow inside its
head. Then it loses
the outside gills.

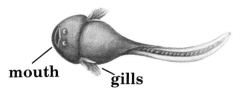

Tadpoles often
start eating tiny
water plants. Later
they may eat small
insects.

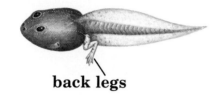

back legs

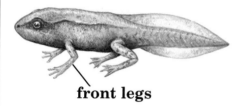

front legs

young frog

The tadpole uses its long tail to swim. It swims around to find food. It swims away from enemies fast.

After a while, back legs grow, then front legs. The tadpole's gills are lost and it develops lungs. Then it can breathe out of the water.

The tail gets shorter and shorter. At last the tadpole turns into a little frog and hops onto land.

It may take two or

three months for the
tadpole to become a frog.

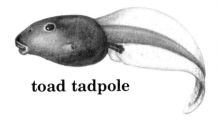

toad tadpole

Other amphibians have
tadpoles too. This toad
tadpole has a large, round
body and a long, strong
tail.

Newt and salamander
"tadpoles" are called
larvae. They grow front
legs first, then back
legs. They do not lose
their tails. They keep
their outside gills for a
long time. Some keep
theirs forever.

newt tadpole

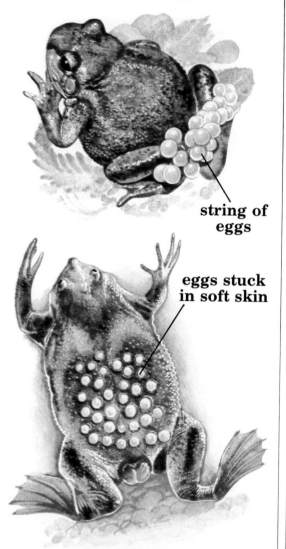

midwife toad

There are toads that do not lay eggs and then leave them. They carry the eggs on their bodies until they hatch.

The male midwife toad puts the eggs on his back legs with a long string of jelly.

The Surinam toad lays her eggs on her back. The eggs stick there. The mother carries them until they turn into toads.

string of eggs

eggs stuck in soft skin

Surinam toad

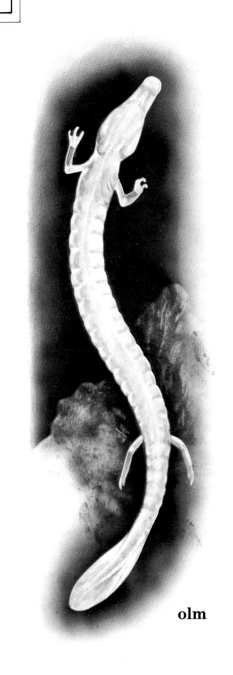

olm

This amphibian never grows up. It has the form of a tadpole all its life.

The olm lives in deep water in caves where it is always dark. It never leaves the water.

It is blind and its skin has no color. The olm cannot stand the sun. If it is put into light, its skin turns dark and it may die.

This is the tadpole of the Mexican salamander. It is called an axolotl. Axolotls live in water. They breathe through gills. Axolotls don't usually develop lungs, so they cannot live long on land. Most axolotls spend all their lives as larvae. They don't grow up. This may be because they do not get enough iodine from what they eat.

axolotl

Axolotls that get enough iodine may grow up. They turn into salamanders that live on land.

Axolotls can lay eggs even though they have not developed completely.

This is another kind of axolotl. It is an albino axolotl. It is pink, with red gills.

albino axolotl

Amphibians were the first animals with backbones to live successfully on land. One amphibian was called Eryops. Eryops lived millions of years ago. It was much bigger than most amphibians that live today. Eryops was a big as some crocodiles.

Eryops

Caecilians are odd amphibians. They look like big worms. Most caecilians live under the ground like worms. They usually come out of the ground at night, especially when it is raining. They have no legs and weak eyes.

caecilian

This is a very strange amphibian. Its tadpole is much bigger than the frog! Instead of growing up to become a big frog, the tadpole shrinks into a tiny frog!

Its name, paradoxical, means unusual or different from normal.

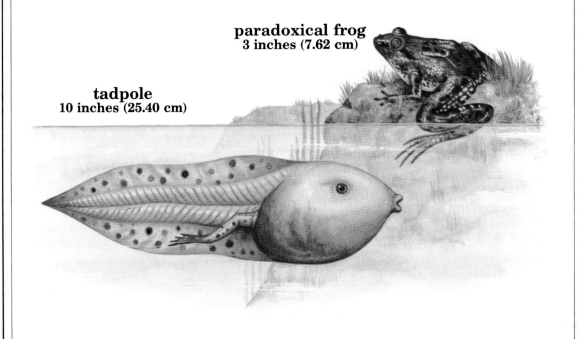

paradoxical frog
3 inches (7.62 cm)

tadpole
10 inches (25.40 cm)

This climbing salamander can go up into the tree tops.

It has long teeth for feeding and fighting its enemies. It can also change its color and may not be seen by its enemies.

Most salamanders have no voice. But this one squeaks like a mouse.

climbing salamander

Amphibians are cold-blooded. That means their bodies are as warm or cold as the air or water around them.

When winter comes, amphibians must find warm homes to stay alive.

Some dig homes in the mud under a pond. Others hide under rocks, dead leaves, or logs. Then they may "sleep" for the winter.

This picture shows several amphibians sleeping. Can you find them?

How a Frog Grows

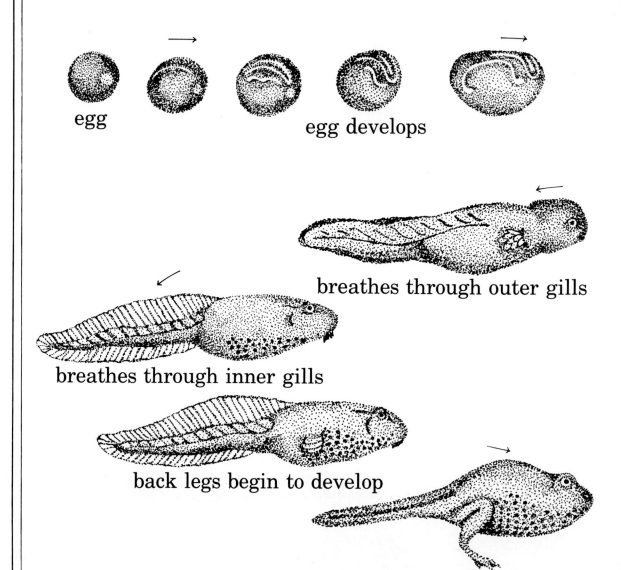

egg

egg develops

breathes through outer gills

breathes through inner gills

back legs begin to develop

back legs grow

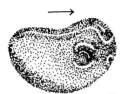

head and body   tail develops

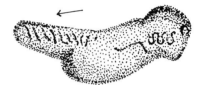

gills grow

egg turns into tadpole

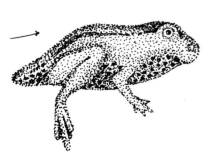

tadpole turns into frog

front legs grow

Where to Read About the Frogs and Toads

Pronunciation Key for Glossary

a	a as in **cat**, **bad**
ā	a as in **able**, ai as in **train**, ay as in **play**
ä	a as in **father**, **car**
e	e as in **bend**, **yet**
ē	e as in **me**, ee as in **feel**, ea as in **beat**, ie as in **piece**, y as in **heavy**
i	i as in **in**, **pig**
ī	i as in **ice**, **time**, ie as in **tie**, y as in **my**
o	o as in **top**
ō	o as in **old**, oa as in **goat**, ow as in **slow**, oe as in **toe**
ô	o as in **cloth**, au as in **caught**, aw as in **paw**, a as in **all**
oo	oo as in **good**, u as in **put**
o͞o	oo as in **tool**, ue as in **blue**
oi	oi as in **oil**, oy as in **toy**
ou	ou as in **out**, ow as in **plow**
u	u as in **up**, **gun**, o as in **other**
ur	ur as in **fur**, er as in **person**, ir as in **bird**, or as in **work**
yo͞o	u as in **use**, ew as in **few**
ə	a as in **again**, e as in **broken**, i as in **pencil**, o as in **attention**, u as in **surprise**
ch	ch as in **such**
ng	ng as in **sing**
sh	sh as in **shell**, **wish**
th	th as in **three**, **bath**
<u>th</u>	th as in **that**, **together**

GLOSSARY

These words are defined the way they are used in this book.

amphibian (am fib′ ē ən) a moist-skinned, cold-blooded animal with a backbone and usually without scales that lives both on land and in the water

attack (ə tak′) to begin to fight against an enemy or prey

backbone (bak′ bōn′) the spine; bones in the back of a person or animal that support the body

blind (blīnd) not able to see

body (bod′ ē) the whole of an animal or plant

breathe (brēth) to take air into the body and send it back out

bumpy (bum′ pē) not smooth; having lumps

burrowing (bur′ ō ing) digging into the ground

cannot (kan′ ot *or* ka not′) is not able; can not

cave (kāv) a natural hollow place in the ground or in the side of a mountain

claw (klô) a sharp, curved nail on an animal's foot

cloudy (klou′ dē) covered over with clouds

clump (klump) several things in a group or bunch

cold-blooded (kōld′ blud′ id) having a body temperature that changes with the surrounding air or water temperature

colored (kul′ ərd) having color

colorful (kul′ ər fəl) bright with color; not plain

complete (kəm plēt′) whole; all of something

crest (krest) a ridge found on the back of some animals

croak (krōk) the sound a frog makes

crocodile (krok′ ə dīl′) a cold-blooded animal with long, strong jaws, teeth and tail, short legs, and scaly skin

damp (damp) somewhat wet; not dry

dangerous (dān′ jər əs) apt to cause

something bad to happen or someone to be
hurt

develop (di vel′ əp) to grow and change in
a natural way

especially (es pesh′ ə lē) more than is
usual

female (fē′ māl) of the sex that gives
birth to young or produces eggs

float (flōt) to rest on top of water
or to move slowly through air or water

flow (flō) to move along smoothly

forever (fə rev′ ər) always; without an end

form (fôrm) to take shape

frill (fril) a curly edge, like a ruffle

gill (gil) the part of a fish or water
animal used for breathing

gland (gland) a part of a body used to
make something the body needs or
something the body gives off

grown (grōn) become as large as something
is supposed to

horned (hôrnd) having a pointed growth on
the head

insect (in′ sekt) a small animal without a backbone, such as a fly or ant

iodine (ī′ ə dīn′ *or* ī′ ə dēn′) a chemical element

itself (it self′) that same one

jelly (jel′ ē) a soft, firm substance that is often clean

larva (lär′ və) the wormlike form of an insect after it hatches from an egg *plural* **larvae**

larvae see **larva**

log (lôg *or* log) a piece of the trunk or a branch of a tree, cut at each end with the bark still on

lose (lōoz) to miss something from its usual place

lung (lung) one of two organs in an animal's chest used for breathing

male (māl) of the sex that can father young

marsh (märsh) soft, low, wet land

Mexican (mek′ si kən) of or having to do with the country of Mexico

million (mil′ yən) the number 1,000,000

newt (no͞ot *or* nyo͞ot) a small salamander that lives in or near water

normal (nôr′ məl) what is usual

odd (od) strange

onto (ôn′ to͞o *or* on′ to͞o) to a place on top or above

padded (pad′ id) having a soft covering

pink (pingk) a color that is a mixture of red and white

poison (poi′ zən) something that can cause sickness or death

pool (po͞ol) a body of water smaller than a lake

rough (ruf) not smooth or level; having bumps

sac (sak) a bag-shaped part of a plant or animal which often holds a liquid

salamander (sal′ ə man′ dər) a lizardlike fresh-water animal

shrink (shringk) to get smaller in size

skin (skin) the outer covering of a person's or animal's body

slippery (slip′ ər ē) causing something or someone to slide

smooth (smōo͞th) not rough; even or level

snore (snôr) to breathe with a harsh sound while sleeping

space (spās) all the room within an area

spawn (spôn) the eggs laid by frogs, fish, and some other water animals

split (split) to break into two or more parts

squeak (skwēk) a thin, high sound made by some animals

sticky (stik′ ē) causing something to be held fast or unable to move easily

stretchy (strech′ ē) able to be made longer or larger by pulling

successfully (sək ses′ fəl lē) done in a way that something turns out as it is supposed to

sucker (suk′ ər) a part of an animal's body that lets it hold onto something

sunny (sun′ ē) lighted and warmed by the sun

swell (swel) to get larger; to puff up

tadpole (tad' pōl') the form of a frog
or toad when it lives in the water and
has not yet grown legs

throat (thrōt) a small opening in
the body between the mouth and
the stomach through which food passes

toad (tōd) a froglike animal that spends
more time on land than in the water

tongue (tung) a movable part of the
mouth used for tasting and swallowing

trunk (trungk) the main part of a tree
from which the branches grow

wart (wôrt) a hard, small lump that
may grow on the skin of an animal
like the toad

weak (wēk) not strong

Bibliography

Allen, Gertrude E. *Everyday Turtles, Toads, and Their Kin*. Boston: Houghton Mifflin Company, 1970.

Burton, Maurice, and Burton, Robert, editors. *The International Wildlife Encyclopedia*. 20 vols. Milwaukee: Purnell Reference Books, 1970.

Knobler, Susan. *The Tadpole and the Frog*. Chippewa Falls, Wis.: Harvey House, 1974.

Naden, Corinne J. *Let's Find Out About Frogs*. New York: Franklin Watts, 1972.
An easy-to-read description of the physical characteristics and behavior of frogs.

Ommanney, F. D. *Frogs, Toads and Newts*. New York: McGraw-Hill Book Company, 1975.

Ridout, Ronald, and Holt, Michael. *Frogs*. New York: Grosset and Dunlap, 1974.

Selsam, Millicent E., and Hunt, Joyce. *A First Look at Frogs, Toads and Salamanders*. New York: Walker and Company, 1976.

Simon, Hilda. *Frogs and Toads of the World*. Philadelphia: J. B. Lippincott Company, 1975.

Simon, Seymour. *Discovering What Frogs Do*. New York: McGraw-Hill Book Company, 1969.
Describes the habits and habitats of frogs, their maturation process, and their anatomy. Includes instructions on starting and maintaining an aquarium.

Turner, Edward, and Turner, Clive. *Frogs and Toads.*
Edited by Barbara Brenner. Milwaukee:
Raintree Publishers Limited, 1976.
This book describes the lives of the different
kinds of frogs and toads throughout the
world — their development from the earliest
amphibians, their lives and habits, and
how they adapt to their surroundings.